Shapes

Circles

by Sarah L. Schuette

Reading Consultant:

Elena Bodrova, Ph.D., Senior Consultant

Mid-continent Research for Education and Learning

an imprint of Capstone Press

Mankato, Minnesota

A+ Books are published by Capstone Press,
P.O. Box 669, 151 Good Counsel Drive, Mankato, Minnesota 56002.
www.capstonepress.com

122009
005645R

Library of Congress Cataloging-in-Publication Data
Schuette, Sarah L., 1976–
    Circles / by Sarah L. Schuette.
    p.cm—(Shapes)
    Summary: Simple text, photographs, and illustrations show circles in everyday objects and actions. Includes bibliographical references and index.
    ISBN-13: 978-0-7368-1460-7 (hardcover)
    ISBN-10: 0-7368-1460-4 (hardcover)
    ISBN-13: 978-0-7368-5058-2 (paperback)
    ISBN-10: 0-7368-5058-9 (paperback)
    I. Circle—Juvenile literature. [1.Circle.] I. Title.
QA484 .S383 2003
516'.15—dc21   2002000894

Created by the A+ Team

Sarah L. Schuette, editor; Heather Kindseth, art director and designer; Jason Knudson, designer and illustrator; Angi Gahler, illustrator; Gary Sundermeyer, photographer; Nancy White, photo stylist

Note to Parents, Teachers, and Librarians
The Shapes series uses color photographs and a nonfiction format to introduce children to the shapes around them. It is designed to be read aloud to a pre-reader or to be read independently by an early reader. Images and activities help early readers and listeners understand the text and concepts discussed. The book encourages further learning by including the following sections: Table of Contents, Words to Know, Read More, Internet Sites, and Index. Early readers may need assistance using these features.

Table of Contents

Circles are shapes
flat and round.

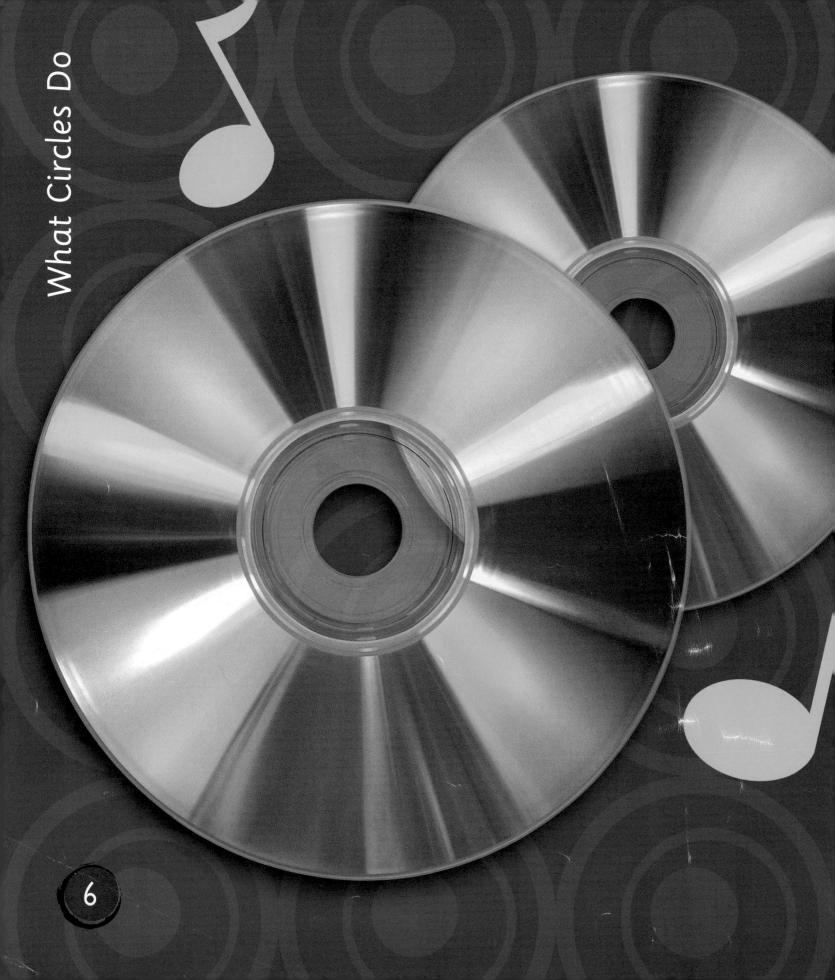

Compact disc (CD) players read CDs from the inside out. The first song on a CD is recorded near the center.

Circles spin to make a sound.

A wheel is a machine just like
a computer or a lawn mower.
Machines make work easier.
Cars cannot move without wheels.

Circles are wheels that roll on the streets.

9

Coins are circles you
save to buy treats.

A flying circle
flips and dips.

Pods growing on the cacao tree have beans inside. These beans can be made into chocolate chips, candy bars, and hot chocolate.

Cookies are circles with chocolate chips.

Dolls have eyes
with circles inside.

Your blinking eyelids act like windshield wipers. They protect your eyes from dirt and dust floating around in the air.

17

Ride this circle and swing out wide.

Circles hold air
and float on a lake.

This tasty circle
is a pancake.

Candy circles taste sweet and sour.

The taste buds on your tongue tell you if foods are sweet, sour, salty, or bitter. But without your nose, you cannot taste flavors such as chocolate or watermelon.

Find the circle that tells you the hour.

Make a Circle Shaker

You will need

2 paper plates

small cup of unpopped
popcorn kernels

stapler

markers or crayons

1 Flip one plate so that the back is facing you. Put it on top of the other paper plate.

2 Staple the edges of the two plates together about half way around the plates. Make sure the staples are very close together.

3 Pour the popcorn into the hole and staple the rest of the edges together.

4 Decorate the circle shaker with circles and shake to see what sounds you can make.

Words to Know

machine—an object that makes work easier; wheels are simple machines; lawn mowers are complex machines.

pod—a long case that holds seeds or beans

taste bud—one of the clusters of cells on the tongue that senses whether something is sweet, sour, bitter, or salty; people are born with about 10,000 taste buds; some taste buds die as people age.

tongue—the movable muscle in your mouth that is used for tasting, talking, and swallowing; the tongue is the largest muscle in your head.

Read More

Baranski, Joan Sullivan. *Round Is a Pancake.* New York: Dutton Children's Books, 2001.

Dotlich, Rebecca Kai. *What Is Round?* New York: Harper Festival, 1999.

Salzmann, Mary Elizabeth. *Circles.* What Shape Is It? Edina, Minn.: ABDO, 2000.

Thong, Roseanne. *Round Is a Mooncake: A Book of Shapes.* San Francisco: Chronicle Books, 2000.

Internet Sites

Track down many sites about circles.
Visit the FACT HOUND at *http://www.facthound.com*

IT IS EASY! IT IS FUN!

1) Go to *http://www.facthound.com*
2) Type in: 0736814604
3) Click on "FETCH IT" and FACT HOUND will find several links hand-picked by our editors.

Relax and let our pal FACT HOUND do the research for you!

Index